NINJA FOODI

COOKBOOK

AIR FRYER

7200 Days of Making Memorable, Mouthwatering Family Meals

THE BRITISH

BY: SOPHIE WATSON

Table of Contents

BREAKFAST

LUNCH

POULTRY

MEAT

SEAFOOD

SIDE DISH

32 Pumpkin Fries

33 Delicious Asparagus

34 Crispy Kale Chips

35 Air-Fried Radishes

36 Buffalo Cauliflower

STARTERS

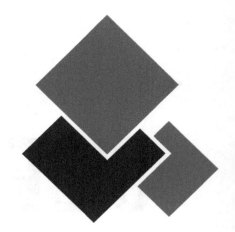

VEGETABLE

DESSERTS

Breakfast
Recipes

Chapter: 1

Tasty Pizookie

Preparation Steps:

1. Begin by preheating the ninja air fryer to 175 degrees C.
2. For making a little dish out of aluminium foil, fold the four sides inwards.
3. Install a piece of your cookie dough in the heart of the foil, then place the other cookie dough pieces around it in a pattern resembling the cube's five sides.
4. In the ninja air fryer, bake the cookie for around six minutes.
5. Open the ninja air fryer and gently press down the top of the cookie, then continue the baking process until it becomes deeply golden brown, for an additional 2 to 4 minutes. Add gelato, whipped cream, and a sprinkle of chocolate that has been melted last.
6. Serve and savour!

Ingredients:

 Prep + Cooking Time: 15 mins

 Portions: 6

- Five pieces of pre-cut refrigerated chocolate chip cookie dough
- One scoop of vanilla gelato
- 30g whipped cream, or as needed
- 30g chocolate, melted, to drizzle

Pancakes

Preparation Steps:

1. Combine the baking powder and flour together in a medium bowl. Meanwhile, combine egg, 30ml vegetable oil, and milk in a large bowl.
2. Try to make a smooth batter by Stirring both mixtures of flour and milk. After approximately a minute, set aside to let the batter thicken.
3. Heat your pan that matches your ninja air fryer with 5ml of the oil for 1 min over medium heat.
4. Use a large spoonful to drop the batter into your ninja air fryer pan, then add the blueberries, and cook for between three and four minutes, or until bubbles appear and the edges are dry.
5. Flip and continue the cooking for around 2 to 3 mins or until golden on the other side.
6. Repeat that with the last batter and oil.

 Prep + Cooking Time: 25 mins

 Portions: 6

Ingredients:

- 155g cups flour
- 15g baking powder
- 185ml whole milk
- An egg
- 45ml vegetable oil, divided
- Half a cup of blueberries, or more to taste

Delicious Waffle Egg in a Hole

Preparation Steps:

1. Heat your ninja air fryer to 175 degrees C.
2. Make a hole in the centre of the frozen waffle with a cup's rim, then put it within the parchment paper square.
3. In the preheated ninja air fryer, carefully put the parchment paper along with the small centre waffle.
4. Next, try to crack the egg directly into the middle of the waffle hole with a little pepper and salt to taste.
5. When the egg white starts to set after roughly five to six mins of cooking.
6. Take the waffle outta the ninja air fryer and start topping it with shredded cheese.
7. Keep cooking for an additional one to two minutes, or until the egg white is fully set and the cheese has melted.
8. Move the egg waffle onto a dish, drizzle it with maple syrup, and prefer to serve it immediately.

  Prep + Cooking Time: 10 mins

Portions:8

Ingredients:

- One frozen waffle
- A large egg
- Salt and pepper to taste
- 10g shredded cheese
- Maple syrup to taste

Fried Eggs

Preparation Steps:

1. Preheat your air fyre to 193°C.
2. Form the foil piece into a circular form, letting the bottom flat and the edges curled inward to create a bowl.
3. Coat the bottom of the bowl with nonstick cooking spray.
4. Inside the drawer of the fryer device, place the foil bowl.
5. Meanwhile, start to break an egg in the middle of the foil. Cook for a total of four minutes.
6. Take the foil bowl away from the drawer and season with pepper and salt to your liking. Serve and enjoy!

Ingredients:

 Prep + Cooking Time: 6 mins

 Portions: 6

- A piece of aluminium foil (4x5 inches)
- cooking spray
- A large egg
- salt and freshly ground black pepper to taste

Chili and Parsley Soufflé

Preparation Steps:

1. Combine all elements in a bowl and whisk well, then pour the mixture into three ramekins.
2. Transfer the ramekins to your ninja air fryer's drawer and cook at 205°C for roughly nine minutes. It prefers to serve immediately.
3. Enjoy!

 Prep + Cooking Time: 9 mins

 Portions: 2

Ingredients:

- Three eggs
- One chopped red chilli pepper
- 30ml Double cream
- 8g finely chopped parsley
- Salt & white pepper

Apple Oatmeal

Preparation Steps:

1. Start by spraying your ninja air fryer machine with cooking spray, and then add all of the ingredients and stir.
2. Coat and begin the cooking process at 180°C for around a quarter-hour.
3. Divide into bowls and serve.

 Prep + Cooking Time: 15 mins

 Portions: 3

Ingredients:

- 200g steel-cut oats
- 730ml almond milk
- Two apples; cored, peeled and chopped
- 8g vanilla extract
- 10g sugar
- 1.5g cinnamon powder
- 0.5g ground nutmeg
- 0.5g ground allspice
- 0.5g ginger powder
- 0.5g ground cardamom
- Cooking spray

Lunch
Recipes

Chapter: 2

Delicious Reuben Sandwich

Preparation Steps:

1. Spread Thousand Island dressing equally on one side of the bread slices, then a layer of one piece of Swiss cheese, followed by two slices of corned beef, add a quarter-cup of sauerkraut, and one more slice of Swiss cheese on four slices of bread.
2. Place the remaining bread pieces on top, coating side down. Top each sandwich with butter. Inside the preheated ninja air fryer,
3. Fill the drawer with sandwiches. Coat the top of each sandwich with the rest of the butter.
4. Cook until both surfaces are golden brown, roughly five minutes per side.
5. Serve while still heated.

 Prep + Cooking Time: 5 mins

 Portions: 5

Ingredients:

- Eight of slices rye bread
- 130g Thousand Island dressing
- Eight slices of Swiss cheese
- Eight slices deli sliced corned beef
- 155g drained sauerkraut
- 30ml softened butter

Homemade Corn Dogs

Preparation Steps:

1. In a medium mixing bowl, combine baking powder, salt, pepper, cornmeal, flour, and sugar; whisk in milk and an egg to produce a batter.
2. Heat your ninja air fryer with oil at 190°C. In the meantime, pat each frankfurter dry and place a skewer into everyone.
3. Roll the frankfurters in the batter until evenly covered.
4. In preheated oil, fry in batches, two or three corn dogs at a time, for roughly three minutes or until lightly browned.
5. Dry with paper towels.
6. Serve and enjoy!!

 Prep + Cooking Time: 40 mins

 Portions: 6

Ingredients:

- 155g yellow cornmeal
- 120g flour
- 50g white sugar
- 20g baking powder
- 0.5g salt
- 0.5g black pepper
- 240ml milk
- An egg
- 1-quart vegetable oil for frying
- Two packages of beef frankfurters
- Sixteen wooden skewers

Chicken and Cabbage Curry

Preparation Steps:

1. Grease a baking dish that fits your ninja air fryer with oil and then add all items; toss.
2. Insert the pan into the fryer and cook at 190°C for a half-hour.
3. Divide among bowls and serve

 Prep + Cooking Time:30 mins

 Portions: 3

Ingredients:

- 680g boneless chicken thighs
- 285ml coconut milk
- One green shredded cabbage
- Two chopped chilli peppers
- A chopped yellow onion
- 125ml apple cider vinegar
- Four minced garlic cloves
- 15ml olive oil
- 45g curry paste
- 15ml soy sauce
- Salt & black pepper

Runner Beans Casserole

Preparation Steps:

1. Begin by greasing a heat-proof dish that fits your ninja air fryer with oil, then add all the elements and toss well.
2. Insert the dish into the fryer and cook at 185°C for around twenty minutes.
3. Divide among plates, serve and enjoy!

  Prep + Cooking Time: 25 mins

Portions: 3

Ingredients:

- 375g trimmed and halved runner beans
- Two red chopped chillies
- 2.5g black mustard seeds
- 25g chopped yellow onion
- Two chopped tomatoes
- Three minced garlic cloves
- 10g tamarind paste
- 1g fenugreek seeds
- 2.5g turmeric powder
- 5ml olive oil
- 5g coriander powder
- 2g chopped coriander
- Salt & black pepper

Tasty Beef Bacon

Preparation Steps:

1. Check that the layers of beef bacon don't overlap while you arrange them in a single layer in the device's drawer. The amount of space in the device drawer influences the number of rashers you can cook at one time.
2. Cook streaky beef bacon rashers in your ninja air fryer set to 200°C for 6–10 mins; shorter cooking times result in crispier beef bacon. To your liking, cook the back beef bacon rashers for 4 to 8 minutes.
3. When frying in batches, keep in mind that after the ninja air fryer has heated up, the second batch will often go faster. employing the tongs to eliminate the beef bacon and set it on kitchen towels to drain before presenting.

Ingredients:

- Six rashers streaky beef bacon, or 3 rashers back beef bacon

 Prep + Cooking Time: 10 mins

 Portions:3

Avocado Fries

Preparation Steps:

1. Turn the ninja air fryer on to 200°C. The egg should be put in a small bowl.
2. Start making a combination of salt, cornmeal, chipotle pepper, and garlic powder in a separate little bowl.
3. Avocado slices should be dipped in eggs, then lightly patted into a cornmeal batter to help them adhere. Avocado slices should be placed in a pregreased tray in the ninja air fryer drawer and sprayed with cooking spray as you go.
4. Cook for approximately four mins or until lightly golden. Toss with cooking spray and turn.
5. Cook for around 3–4 more mins. Avocado slices can be served with salsa, pico de gallo, lime wedges, or ranch dressing if preferred.

 Prep + Cooking Time: 30 mins

 Portions: 5

Ingredients:

- One large egg, beaten
- 40g cornmeal
- 0.5g salt
- 1g garlic powder
- 1g ground chipotle pepper
- Two medium avocados, peeled and sliced
- Cooking spray
- Optional: Lime wedges, salsa, pico de gallo or spicy ranch dressing

Poultry
Recipes

Chapter: 3

Thanksgiving Chicken

Preparation Steps:

1. Take the chicken away from the refrigerator and set it aside for fifteen minutes until it reaches room temperature. If using stuffing, fill your chicken now. If not, add lemon slices and herbs to the cavity.
2. Meantime, truss the chicken. Preheat your ninja air fryer machine to 180°C.
3. In the ninja air fryer, arrange the spiced chicken breast side down. Cook at 180°C for thirty minutes in total. Flip the chicken into the drawer of the device.
4. Cook for an additional twenty minutes at 180°C. Cook for another 5 to 10 minutes if the chicken is stuffed. Once a quick-read temperature in the thickest section of the chicken reaches 75°C, it is done.
5. Leave the chicken to rest for fifteen to twenty minutes before cutting.

  Prep + Cooking Time: 1h 35 mins

Portions: 5

Ingredients:

- 15g Sea salt
- 5g poultry seasoning
- 1g garlic powder
- 1g onion powder
- 2270g whole chicken
- One lemon sliced, fresh herbs, or stuffing (optional)

Apples and Glazed Chicken

Preparation Steps:

1. Begin by heating a pan that fits your frying machine with a tablespoon of oil over medium heat.
2. Then, add the honey, mustard, cider and combine well. Bring to a simmer and take away from the heat.
3. Toss with the remaining ingredients. Move the pan to your fryer device and cook for about 7–10 minutes at 200°C. Serve and enjoy!

 Prep + Cooking Time: 12 mins

 Portions: 5

Ingredients:

- Six chicken thighs; skin-on
- Three cored and sliced apples
- 155ml apple cider
- 30ml olive oil
- 2g chopped rosemary
- 30ml honey
- 15g mustard
- Salt & black pepper

Courgette Mushroom Chicken

Preparation Steps:

1. Make sure the chicken breast is well covered with bicarbonate of soda. Leave for twenty minutes. Make a combination between ginger, garlic, red pepper flakes, rice vinegar, soy sauce, and sugar. Place aside.
2. Take the bicarbonate of soda off the chicken and pat it dry with high-quality paper towels. In a pan that matches your ninja air fryer and over medium-high heat, combine a tablespoon of sesame oil and vegetable oil.
3. When the oil is heated, add the chicken and fry for approximately four minutes or until both surfaces are golden.
4. Eliminate the chicken from the pan. Add the mushrooms, onion, and courgette to the pan with the remaining vegetable oil. Cook for approximately three minutes, stirring regularly, or until the vegetables are softened.
5. After adding the chicken and sauce, stir until the vegetables and poultry are well coated with sauce.
6. Cook for another minute. Serve with white or brown rice.

 Prep + Cooking Time: 30 mins

 Portions: 6

Ingredients:

- 455g chicken breast sliced thinly into bite-sized pieces
- 3g Bicarbonate of soda
- 30ml vegetable oil divided
- 15ml sesame oil
- 65ml soy sauce
- 15ml rice wine vinegar
- 10g white sugar
- 5g garlic minced
- 2g ginger grated
- 1g red pepper flakes optional
- 225g white mushrooms sliced
- A half-medium onion sliced
- One medium courgette cut in half lengthwise then sliced
- salt & pepper

Chicken with Lemon and Garlic

Preparation Steps:

1. Combine all of the items in a bowl and toss well.
2. Put the chicken mixture in your ninja air fryer device and cook at 180°C for roughly a quarter-hour.
3. Serve and enjoy!

 Prep + Cooking Time: 15 mins

 Portions: 3

Ingredients:

- Four skinless and boneless chicken breasts
- Four garlic heads peeled, cloves
- separated and cut into quarters
- 30ml lemon juice
- 2g lemon pepper
- 20ml avocado oil
- Salt & black pepper

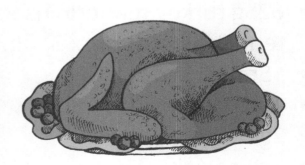

Awesome Turkey Tenderloin

Preparation Steps:

1. Preheat the ninja air fryer devic to 180°C. Turkey tenderloins should be pre-rubbed with poultry spice, olive oil, black pepper, Sea salt, and onion powder or you can rub it at the moment.
2. In the preheated ninja air fryer drawer, Put the turkey tenderloins.
3. Cook tenderloins for approximately 22-25 minutes, or until the meat's internal temperature reaches 75°C.
4. Eliminate it from the ninja air fryer and lay it aside for five to ten minutes on a cutting surface to rest before slicing and serving.

 Prep + Cooking Time: 35 mins

 Portions: 4

Ingredients:

- 625g turkey tenderloins 2 tenderloins, approx 3/4 lb each
- 15ml olive oil
- 10g poultry seasoning
- 2g onion powder
- 5g Sea salt
- 1g black pepper

Chicken Drumsticks

Preparation Steps:

1. Preheat the ninja air fryer to 205°C.
2. Rub the chicken drumsticks with the onion powder, paprika, Light brown sugar, thyme, garlic powder, Sea salt, and black pepper. Let the drumsticks marinate for approximately fifteen to thirty minutes in the seasoning.
3. Into the ninja air fryer drawer in batches, arrange the drumsticks and air fry for about 12 minutes.
4. After the time is completed, open the drawer and turn the drumsticks. Cook for eight to ten minutes more.
5. Take the ninja air fryer drawer away and sprinkle with parsley. Serve and enjoy.

 Prep + Cooking Time: 26 mins

 Portions: 5

Ingredients:

- Eight Chicken drumsticks patted dry
- 2g Garlic powder
- 5g Light Brown sugar
- 2g Paprika
- 1g Thyme
- 1g Onion powder
- 0.5g Black pepper
- 5g Sea salt
- 5g Fresh parsley chopped, for garnish

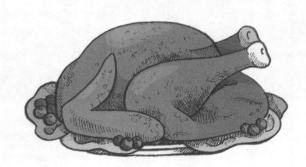

Meat
Recipes

Chapter: 4

Beef Roast

Preparation Steps:

1. If necessary, you can cut the beef roast into slices to fit in the ninja air fryer drawer. To make the rub, mix the garlic powder, pepper, salt, Light brown sugar, paprika, ground mustard, and red pepper flakes in a small bowl.
2. Spread the rub evenly over the beef roast pieces. Install the beef roast in the device's drawer. Leave this to sit for a total of twenty minutes to rest.
3. Next, cook in the ninja air fryer at 190°C for 75-90 minutes, or until the temperature of the meat gets around 96°C. It is nicely done at 60°C, but the closer it comes to 96°C, the more tender it will be.
4. Allow it to rest for about ten mins before slicing and serving.

 Prep + Cooking Time: 2h

 Portions: 4

Ingredients:

- 1815g Boneless Beef Roast Shoulder
- 45g Light Brown Sugar Packed
- 45g Salt
- 1g Pepper
- 2g Paprika
- 2g Crushed Red Pepper Flakes
- 1.5g Ground Mustard
- 1.5g Garlic Powder

Meatloaf (Gluten-Free)

Preparation Steps:

1. Integrate all the meatloaf items in a genius mixing bowl.
2. Use the olive oil cooking spray to spray a sheet of foil before shaping and arranging the meatloaf on it. Roll it up on the sides a little so that it's not completely closed, but air can pass through in the ninja air fryer.
3. Pop it in the Ninja air fryer. Cook for a total of twenty minutes in your ninja air fryer at 200 °C.
4. While it's cooking, put all the sauce components in a small saucepan and whisk until incorporated over medium-low heat. This will take simply a few minutes. After 20 minutes, gently remove the meatloaf from the Ninja air fryer and spritz it with the sauce.
5. Cook for 2 to 5 minutes more, or until the meatloaf reaches an internal temp of 65 °C.
6. Carefully take it off and serve.

 Prep + Cooking Time: 35 mins

 Portions: 6

Ingredients:

- 905g Ground Beef
- Two Beaten Eggs
- 180g Old-Fashioned Oats Regular or Gluten-Free
- 125ml Evaporated Milk
- 25g Chopped Onion
- 1g Garlic Salt

Sauce:

- 235ml Ketchup
- 125g Light Brown Sugar Packed
- 15g Chopped Onion
- 2g Liquid Smoke
- 0.5g Garlic Powder
- Foil
- Olive Oil Cooking Spray

Brats with Beer Gravy

Preparation Steps:

1. Set the ninja air fryer to 205°C. In a greased ninja air fryer, arrange bratwurst in a single layer.
2. Cook for approximately eight to ten mins or until no longer pink. Butter is heated in the meantime over medium-high heat by using a saucepan.
3. Add the onion and toss while cooking it until it begins to turn brown and is tender.
4. Stir in the pepper, dill weed, and flour until smooth. Beer is brought to a boil. Reduce heat; cook for roughly 3–5 mins with constant stirring.
5. Place one brat on each slice of bread before equally spreading the onion mixture on top.

 Prep + Cooking Time: 20 mins

 Portions: 5

Ingredients:

- One package of uncooked bratwurst links
- 30g butter
- A medium onion, thinly sliced
- 30g Plain flour
- 0.5g dill weed
- 0.5g pepper
- A bottle of nonalcoholic beer
- Five slices of thick bread

Lamb and carrots

Preparation Steps:

1. Over medium heat, and by using oil, heat up a pan that matches your ninja air fryer device then put the lamb and let it brown with stirring for approximately 1-2 minutes.
2. After that, start adding all of the remaining items and toss well; cook again for two more minutes
3. Move the pan to your ninja air fryer device and cook at 195°C for 25 minutes.
4. the mixture into bowls and serve.

 Prep + Cooking Time: 30 mins

 Portions: 4

Ingredients:

- 625g ground lamb
- Four minced garlic cloves
- Four grated carrots
- One cup of beef stock
- A chopped yellow onion
- 7ml olive oil
- 15ml Cranberry juice
- 1g smoked paprika
- Salt & black pepper

Fantastic Scotch Eggs

Preparation Steps:

1. Set the ninja air fryer to 205°C. Flatten each sausage chunk, then season with pepper & salt.
2. Each serving should be shaped to fit a peeled hard-boiled egg.
3. Roll in the egg batter, then coat with cornflake crumbs. Set on an oiled tray in the device drawer in a single layer. 12 to 15 mins, flipping the meat halfway through, or until the flesh is no longer pink.
4. Enjoy!!

 Prep + Cooking Time: 15 mins

 Portions: 4

Ingredients:

- 455g bulk beef sausage
- Salt and pepper to taste
- Six hard-boiled large eggs
- A large egg, lightly beaten
- 3/4 cup crushed cornflakes

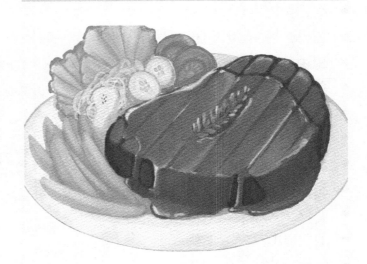

Juicy Meatballs

Preparation Steps:

1. In a medium combining bowl, add everything except the beef and lamb. Mix thoroughly.
2. Join the beef and beef in a mixing bowl. From the resulting mixture into Sixteen meatballs. Heat the ninja air fryer to 205°C.
3. In the ninja air fryer, transfer the meatballs in batches.
4. Change the temperature of the ninja air fryer to 195 °C. Let those meatballs cook for approximately 12–14 minutes, or until they become golden and the inside temperature reaches a maximum of 75 °C.
5. Allow three minutes to rest before serving.

Ingredients:

 Prep + Cooking Time: 20 mins

 Portions: 5

- 455g lean ground beef
- 225g lean ground lamb
- 35g seasoned bread crumbs
- An egg
- 30ml milk
- 10g fresh parsley
- 5g grated parmesan cheese
- 3g Italian seasoning
- 1g onion powder
- 1g salt
- 0.5g black pepper

Seafood
Recipes

Chapter: 5

Breaded Sea Scallops

Preparation Steps:

1. Preheat the ninja air fryer to 198°C.
2. In a small bowl, combine garlic powder, seafood seasoning, and cracker crumbs.
3. In a second shallow container, melt the butter.
4. Begin by dipping each scallop in butter that has been melted, then roll in the breading until thoroughly covered.
5. Repeat with the remaining scallop.
6. Use the cooking spray to spray your ninja air fryer drawer lightly.
7. Arrange the scallops in the prepared drawer so that they do not touch. You may need to work in batches.
8. After preheating the ninja air fryer, Cook until the scallops are opaque, approximately 4 minutes, and flip them halfway to get them equally cooked.

Ingredients:

 Prep + Cooking Time: 10 mins

 Portions: 8

- 180g finely crushed buttery cracker (such as Ritz®)
- 1g garlic powder
- 2g seafood seasoning (such as Old Bay®)
- 30ml melted butter
- 455g sea scallops, patted dry
- cooking spray

Cajun Crab Cakes

Preparation Steps:

1. Preheat the ninja air fryer to 188° C per the manufacturer's instructions.
2. In a small mixing bowl, combine the egg, mayonnaise, cayenne spice, pepper, bread crumbs, Cajun spice, salt, mustard, and Worcestershire sauce. Gently fold in the crabmeat.
3. Using a biscuit cutter, cut out three equal-sized crab cakes.
4. Set the cakes on a baking dish that is already lined with parchment paper and put them gently in the ninja air fryer drawer. Cook for 6 minutes in a hot Ninja air fryer.
5. Cook until golden and coloured on the other side, approximately six minutes longer.
6. Serve on slider buns with remoulade sauce.

Prep + Cooking Time: 13 mins

Portions: 6

Ingredients:

- 90g panko bread crumbs
- 55g mayonnaise
- An egg
- 30ml Worcestershire sauce
- 5g Dijon mustard
- 2g Cajun seasoning
- 3g salt
- 0.5g cayenne pepper
- 0.5g ground white pepper (Optional)
- 115g fresh lump crabmeat
- 45g remoulade sauce, or to taste
- Three brioche slider buns (Optional)

Panko-Crusted Mahi Mahi

Preparation Steps:

1. Preheat the ninja air fryer device to 200°C for five minutes.
2. In the meantime, sprinkle grapeseed oil over mahi mahi fillets on a dish.
3. In a shallow dish, combine garlic salt, bagel seasoning, pepper, panko, and turmeric.
4. Coat each fish in the panko batter before putting it in the drawer of the machine in a single layer. Use the nonstick cooking spray to spray.
5. Cook until the fish flakes easily with a fork in the preheated ninja air fryer, between twelve and fifteen minutes, turning halfway through. Take it out of the ninja air fryer.
6. Garnish with lemon wedges and parsley, if desired. Serve right away.

Ingredients:

 Prep + Cooking Time: 15 mins

 Portions: 6

- 115g mahi mahi fillets
- 30ml grapeseed oil
- 200g panko bread crumbs
- One teaspoon of everything bagel seasoning
- 2g garlic salt
- 2g ground turmeric
- 1g ground black pepper
- nonstick cooking spray
- 1g chopped fresh parsley
- One medium lemon, cut into 4 wedges

Wonderful Pea Pods with Shrimp

Preparation Steps:

1. Combine all of the components in a pan which suits your ninja air fryer device.
2. Position the pan in the fryer and cook for approximately 8 minutes at 190°C.
3. Serve in individual bowls.

 Prep + Cooking Time: 10 mins

 Portions: 3

Ingredients:

- 455g shrimp; peeled and deveined
- 225g pea pods
- 158ml pineapple juice
- 30ml soy sauce
- 45g sugar
- 45ml balsamic vinegar

Mussels and Shrimp

Preparation Steps:

1. Toss all of the components in a pan that suits your ninja air fryer machine.
2. Place the pan in the machine and cook for a quarter-hour at 190°C.
3. Serve immediately in individual bowls.

 Prep + Cooking Time: 16 mins

 Portions: 3

Ingredients:

- 605g large shrimp; peeled and deveined
- 566g chopped canned tomatoes
- 225ml clam juice
- Twelve mussels
- 30ml melted butter
- Two chopped yellow onions
- Three minced garlic cloves
- 15g chopped parsley
- 0.5g dried marjoram
- 2g dried basil
- Salt and black pepper

Crumb-Topped Sole

Preparation Steps:

1. Heat the ninja air fryer device to 190°C. Spread a combination of pepper, mustard seed, two tablespoons of cheese, and mayonnaise over the tops of the fillets.
2. In pregreased tray in the drawer of the device, work in units and put the fish in a single layer. Commence the cooking process for about three to five minutes.
3. Meanwhile, mix the crushed mustard, bread crumbs, onion, and remaining tablespoon of cheese in a small bowl; whisk in the butter.
4. Spoon over fillets, gently massaging to adhere; spritz with cooking spray.
5. Cook until lightly golden and brown, approximately two to three minutes extra.
6. Sprinkle with additional green onions if preferred.

Prep + Cooking Time: 10 mins

Portions: 6

Ingredients:

- 45g reduced-fat mayonnaise
- 20g grated Parmesan cheese, divided
- 5g mustard seed
- 0.5g pepper
- Four sole fillets (6 ounces each)
- 120g soft bread crumbs
- A green onion, finely chopped
- 0.5g ground mustard
- 30ml melted butter
- Cooking spray

Side Dish
Recipes

Chapter: 6

Hash Browns

Preparation Steps:

1. Heat the fryer machine to 190°C.
2. Mix the first Eight items in a large mixing bowl; if wanted, add spicy sauce.
3. Spread the batter in an even 3/4-inch layer on a greased tray in the drawer of the fryer machine and work in batches.
4. Cook for around fifteen to twenty mins, or until brown and crispy. Just before serving, top with parsley.

 Prep + Cooking Time: 20 mins

 Portions: 4

Ingredients:

- One package (30 ounces) of frozen shredded hash brown potatoes
- One large red onion, finely chopped
- One small sweet red pepper, finely chopped
- One small green pepper, finely chopped
- Four minced garlic cloves
- 30ml olive oil
- 0.5g salt
- 0.5g pepper
- Three drops of hot pepper sauce, optional
- 2.5g minced fresh parsley

Pumpkin Fries

Preparation Steps:

1. Marge the chipotle peppers, 1/8 teaspoon salt, maple syrup, and yoghurt in a shallow bowl. Refrigerate, covered, until ready to serve.
2. Heat up the ninja air fryer device to 205°C. Peel the pumpkin and split it in half lengthwise.
3. Save the seeds for toasting or discard them. Pumpkins must be cut into 1/2-inch strips.
4. Switch to a large mixing bowl. Toss with the remaining 1/2 teaspoon salt, cumin, pepper, garlic powder, and chilli powder.
5. Arrange the pumpkin on a pregreased tray in the drawer of the device in batches. 6–8 minutes, or until barely tender.
6. Toss to redistribute; cook till crispy and golden, another 3-5 minutes. Serve with a dipping sauce.

Ingredients:

  Prep + Cooking Time: 20 mins

Portions: 6

- 140g plain Greek yoghurt
- 30ml maple syrup
- Two to Three teaspoons of minced chipotle peppers in adobo sauce
- 1.5g plus
- 3g salt, divided
- One medium pie pumpkin
- 1g garlic powder
- 1g ground cumin
- 1g chilli powder
- 1g pepper

Delicious Asparagus

Preparation Steps:

1. Heat the ninja air fryer device to 190°C.
2. Put the first six elements in a large mixing bowl and combine well.
3. After that, add the asparagus and toss until coated.
4. Working in stages, put them in the drawer of the ninja air fryer device on a pre-greased tray.
5. Cook for roughly four to six mins, or until tender and gently coloured and browned.
6. Place on a serving plate and top with Parmesan cheese. Serve with lemon wedges if preferred.

 Prep + Cooking Time: 20 mins

 Portions: 6

Ingredients:

- 55g mayonnaise
- 20ml olive oil
- 1.5g grated lemon zest
- One minced garlic clove
- 1g pepper
- 1g seasoned salt
- 455g trimmed fresh asparagus
- 10g shredded Parmesan cheese
- Lemon wedges, optional

Crispy Kale Chips

Preparation Steps:

1. Start by heating the ninja air fryer to 190°C. Remove the stiff kale stems and break the leaves into big pieces. Place it in a large mixing basin.
2. Massage olive oil into the leaves to coat them evenly. Season the greens with pepper and salt. Lay the leaves in a single layer on a greased tray in the air-fryer drawer in batches.
3. Cook for around five to seven minutes in total or until crisp and beginning to brown.
4. Allow at least five minutes before serving.

 Prep + Cooking Time: 10 mins

 Portions: 4

Ingredients:

- One bunch kale, washed
- 30ml olive oil
- One to Three teaspoons of seafood seasoning
- Sea salt, to taste

Air-Fried Radishes

Preparation Steps:

1. Heat the ninja air fryer to 190°C.
2. Toss the radishes with the rest of the items. Arrange the radishes in the ninja air fryer drawer on an oiled tray.
3. Cook, stirring occasionally, for approximately twelve to fifteen minutes or until crisp-tender.

 Prep + Cooking Time: 25 mins

 Portions: 3

Ingredients:

- 600g radishes, trimmed and quartered
- 45ml olive oil
- 5g minced fresh oregano
- 0.5g salt
- 0.25g pepper

Buffalo Cauliflower

Preparation Steps:

1. Prepare the ninja air fryer at a temperature of 205°C. Toss the cauliflower in the oil. Set it in your ninja air fryer drawer on a tray.
2. Cook until soft and takes the brown colour, 15-20 minutes, moving halfway while you cook it.
3. Toss with wing sauce in a serving dish. Deliver with dressing.

Prep + Cooking Time: 20 mins

Portions: 3

Ingredients:

- One medium head cauliflower, cut into florets
- 15ml rapeseed oil
- 125ml Buffalo wing sauce
- Blue cheese salad dressing

Starter
Recipes

Chapter: 7

SNACK

Corn On The Cob

Preparation Steps:

1. If required you can use both zones, begin by arranging the corn in an air-fryer drawer in a single layer.
2. Cook at 205°C for approximately ten to twelve minutes, rotating halfway through, until shining golden and tender.
3. At the same time, in a medium mixing bowl, combine the onion, feta, oregano, and basil.
4. Top each cob with two tablespoons of yoghurt and the feta combination.
5. Garnish with paprika and extra basil if desired. With lemon wedges on the side, serve warm or at room temperature.

Ingredients:

 Prep + Cooking Time:25 mins

 Portions: 5

- Four ears of corn, shucked, halved if necessary
- 150g finely crumbled feta
- 10g finely chopped red onion
- 1g finely chopped fresh basil, plus more for serving
- 1g dried oregano
- 110g full-fat plain Greek yoghurt
- 1g sweet or smoked paprika
- Lemon wedges, for serving

Page: 37

Creamy potatoes

Preparation Steps:

1. In a baking dish which suits your ninja air fryer machine, mix all the elements and toss well.
2. Insert the dish into the device and cook at 190°C for around 20 minutes. Divide among plates and serve as a side dish.

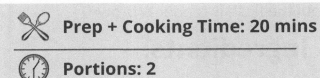

Prep + Cooking Time: 20 mins

Portions: 2

Ingredients:

- Two gold potatoes; cut into medium pieces
- 45ml sour cream
- 15ml olive oil
- Salt and black pepper to taste

Acorn Squash

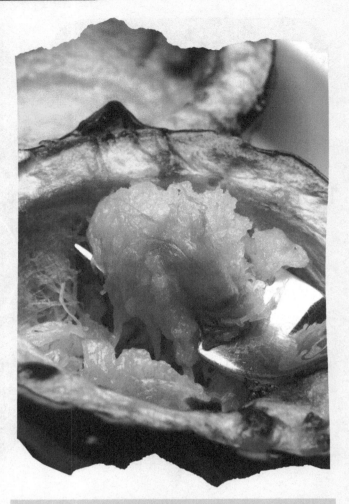

Preparation Steps:

1. Preheat the ninja air fryer device to 190° C.
2. Use a spoon to scrape the seeds out after cutting the squash in half. Season the squash with salt after brushing it with olive oil.
3. Inside the ninja air fryer drawer, and after cutting the side up, cook for 15 minutes.
4. Mix the Light brown sugar, cinnamon, and melted butter while the squash is cooking.
5. When the timer is complete, brush with the Light brown sugar mixture.
6. Cook for roughly ten to fifteen mins, or until the flesh is tender & brown.

 Prep + Cooking Time: 40 mins

 Portions: 6

Ingredients:

- Two small or medium acorn squash
- 15ml olive oil
- 0.5g Sea salt or to taste
- 15ml butter melted
- 15g Light brown sugar
- 0.5g cinnamon

Rosemary Shrimp Kabobs

Preparation Steps:

1. In a bowl, put and toss all the items well.
2. On a skewer, thread two pepper slices and two shrimp, and then repeat that again with two more shrimp and pepper slices.
3. On the other skewer, thread another two pepper slices and two shrimp, and then repeat with the last two pepper slices and two shrimp.
4. Place the kabobs in the fryer's drawer and cook at 180°C for around seven mins.
5. Serve and enjoy!

 Prep + Cooking Time: 10 mins

 Portions: 3

Ingredients:

- Eight peeled and deveined shrimp
- Eight red pepper slices
- Four minced garlic cloves
- 2g chopped rosemary
- 15ml olive oil
- Salt & black pepper

Beef Bacon Wrapped Brussels Sprouts

Preparation Steps:

1. Preheat the ninja air fryer machine to a temp of 190 °C.
2. Trim and wash Brussels sprouts and you have the choice if you want to cut them in half if you see they are big. Wrap each slice of beef bacon around a sprout in thirds.
3. Prepare the drawer with parchment paper (but do not preheat it). Set the drawer seam side down and sprinkle with Light brown sugar.
4. Rep with the remaining Brussels and beef bacon.
5. Bake for a total of a quarter-hour, or until the sprouts are soft and the beef bacon becomes crispy.

Ingredients:

- 455g beef bacon
- 625g brussels sprouts
- 85g Light brown sugar

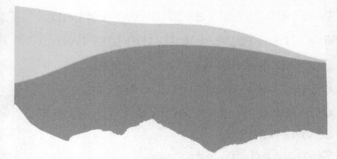

 Prep + Cooking Time: 27 mins

 Portions: 5

tasty Lentils Spread

Preparation Steps:

1. Stir together all the elements in a pan which suits your ninja air fryer.
2. Set the pan in the fryer device and cook for approximately twenty minutes in total at 190°C.
3. Employing an immersion blender, blend this mixture.
4. Serve as a snack or appetiser in individual bowls.

Ingredients:

Prep + Cooking Time: 18 mins

Portions: 4

- 850g crushed canned tomatoes
- 200ml chicken stock
- 380g drained canned red lentils
- Three minced garlic cloves
- Salt & black pepper

Vegetable
Recipes

Chapter: 8

Crispy Garlic Broccoli

Preparation Steps:

1. Heat the ninja air fryer to 205°C.
2. Mix broccoli, garlic, olive oil, and cheese in a lidded container until equally covered.
3. Any remaining cheese should be pressed over the broccoli florets. Season as you like with pepper & salt.
4. Cook for about 5-7 minutes, or until the broccoli gets the desired texture, in a single layer in the ninja air fryer.

 Prep + Cooking Time: 12 mins

 Portions: 4

Ingredients:

- 225g broccoli washed, dried and cut into bite-sized pieces
- 15ml olive oil
- 10g grated parmesan cheese
- One minced clove of garlic
- Sea salt & pepper to taste

Roasted Sweet Potatoes & Carrots

Preparation Steps:

1. Begin by heating the ninja air fryer to 205°C. In a mixing bowl, marge all of the components except the butter.
2. Place in an already-heated ninja air fryer. Simmer for five minutes. Sauté for a further 4-7 minutes, or until gently browned and tender.
3. To serve, toss with butter.

Ingredients:

 Prep + Cooking Time: 15 mins

 Portions: 3

- 135g sweet potatoes peeled and diced 1"
- Three large carrots peeled and sliced
- 15ml olive oil
- 0.5g each salt & pepper
- 0.5g ground cinnamon
- 0.5g ground ginger
- 15g Light brown sugar optional
- 15g butter

Incredible Runner Beans

Preparation Steps:

1. First, the runner beans should be washed and trimmed. Pat dry.
2. Season runner beans with salt and pepper after tossing with olive oil.
3. In a preheated ninja air fryer machine at 200°C, cook your runner beans for 9–11 minutes, shaking the drawer halfway through.
4. Serve & enjoy!!

 Prep + Cooking Time: 12 mins

 Portions: 4

Ingredients:

- 455g runner beans
- 15ml olive oil
- Salt & black pepper to taste

Baked Potatoes

Preparation Steps:

1. Clean potatoes under running water and pat dry. Poke each potato many times with a fork.
2. Season with salt and gently rub with oil. Heat up the ninja air fryer machine to 200 °C.
3. Let it cook for twenty-five minutes, then flip the potatoes and simmer for another 20-30 minutes, until they become tender when pricked with a fork.
4. Serve with chosen garnishes.

Ingredients:

- Four medium russet potatoes
- 15ml olive oil
- Sea salt to taste

Prep + Cooking Time: 50 mins

Portions: 4

Spinach Feta Turnovers

Preparation Steps:

1. Set the ninja air fryer machine to 205°C.
2. Whisk the eggs in a bowl; save a single tablespoon of the mixture. garlic, Spinach, pepper, feta cheese, and the remaining beaten eggs should all be combined.
3. Create a 12-inch square out of the unrolled pizza dough. Four 6-inch squares should be cut out.
4. Add roughly 1/3 cup of the spinach mixture to each square.
5. Trim the edges with a pinch after folding them into triangles.
6. The tops are slitted, and a tablespoon of the egg is brushed on.
7. Triangles should be placed on a greased tray in the ninja air fryer drawer in a single layer, if possible in batches.
8. Cook for around 10 to 12 mins, until lightly golden & coloured brown. Serve with tzatziki sauce if you like it better.

 Prep + Cooking Time: 30 mins

 Portions: 8

Ingredients:

- Two large eggs
- One package of frozen spinach, thawed, squeezed dry and chopped
- 168g crumbled feta cheese
- Two garlic cloves, minced
- 1g pepper
- One tube refrigerated pizza crust
- Refrigerated tzatziki sauce, optional

Yummy Aubergine

Preparation Steps:

1. Toss all of the elements together in a pan which suits your ninja air fryer.
2. Insert the pan into the device and fry for an additional quarter-hour at 205°C.
3. Serve and enjoy!

Ingredients:

 Prep + Cooking Time: 15 mins

 Portions: 3

- Four roughly cubed aubergines
- 15ml olive oil
- 15ml lime juice
- 1g dried oregano
- Salt & black pepper

Dessert
Recipes

Chapter: 9

Cherry Cheesecake Egg Rolls

Preparation Steps:

1. In a mixing container, add lemon juice, sugar, lemon rind, and melted cream cheese.
2. Fill a Ziploc baggie halfway with the mixture.
3. Cut the bag's corner off. Pipe a line of the cheese combination across the egg roll wrapper, pointing one of the corners towards you.
4. Approximately 10 cherries should be placed on top of the cheese mixture.
5. Wet the wrapper's edges and roll it up tightly, making sure the edges are securely sealed. Allow the rolls to sit for three to four minutes to allow the water to dry and form a good seal.
6. Preheat the oil to 175°C and fry in small batches for 5-6 minutes or until golden and crispy.
7. Serve hot.

Ingredients:

Prep + Cooking Time: 25 mins

Portions: 7

- 115g cream cheese softened
- 5ml lemon rind
- 45g sugar
- 7ml lemon juice
- A can of cherry pie filling
- Eight egg roll wrappers mine were 6"x6"
- Oil for frying

Tasty Taquitos

Preparation Steps:

1. Mix the chicken, taco seasoning, and three tablespoons of water in a mixing bowl.
2. Cook for a maximum of five minutes, or until the water has evaporated. Mix in the green onion whites, cream cheese, and jalapenos.
3. Simmer till the cheese has become melted & creamy.
4. Microwave tortillas for 40 seconds, or until warm, on a platter covered with a moist paper towel. Top the tortillas with the contents and 30g of cheese. Roll firmly and use a toothpick to fasten.
5. Heat the Ninja air fryer to 205°C. Taquitos should be brushed with oil or sprayed with frying spray.
6. Cook in a single layer for about 6 to 8 mins, or until crisp.
7. Allow for 2 minutes of cooling before serving.
8. Garnish with the remaining green onions and toppings, if preferred.

 Prep + Cooking Time: 55 mins

 Portions: 8

Ingredients:

- 280g cooked chicken or beef or beef, shredded
- 15g taco seasoning
- 115g cream cheese
- One tablespoon jalapenos finely diced
- One green onion sliced, green and whites divided
- 85g shredded Tex-Mex cheese
- Eight corn tortillas 6 inches each
- Cooking spray

Yammy Yoghurt Cake

Preparation Steps:

1. In a bowl, add all of the items (excluding the cooking spray) and toss thoroughly.
2. Use the cooking spray to grease the cake pan before pouring the batter into the ninja air fryer.
3. Cook for an additional thirty minutes at 165°C.
4. Allow to cool before serving

Prep + Cooking Time: 30 mins

Portions: 4

Ingredients:

- 225g canned pumpkin puree
- A mashed banana
- An egg
- 180g white flour
- 285g Greek yoghurt
- 150g sugar
- 5g Bicarbonate of soda
- 2g vanilla extract
- 2g baking powder
- 30ml vegetable oil
- Cooking spray

Easy Doughnuts

Preparation Steps:

1. Heat the Ninja air fryer device to 175°C.
2. Using a small 1" cutter, cut a circle out of the centre of each cookie.
3. In the ninja air fryer, place 4-5 pieces of dough. Bake for three minutes.
4. Cook for further two or three minutes, or until golden.
5. Eliminate from the ninja air fryer and brush with butter while still heated.
6. Inside the cinnamon-sugar combination toss the doughnuts.
7. Repeat with the rest of the doughnuts.
8. Once the doughnuts are done, place the doughnut holes in the Ninja air fryer for approximately three minutes.
9. If desired, toss with more butter and sugar.

 Prep + Cooking Time: 15 mins

 Portions: 9

Ingredients:

- One can biscuits
- 55g melted butter
- 100g sugar
- 10g cinnamon

Strawberry Cream

Preparation Steps:

1. Use the blender to thoroughly mix all of the elements.
2. Transfer the mixture to six ramekins and set them in the ninja air fryer machine.
3. Cook an additional quarter-hour at 165°C.
4. Serve

Prep + Cooking Time: 15 mins

Portions: 4

Ingredients:

- 225g cream cheese
- 115g strawberries
- 170g Double cream
- 30ml water
- 7ml lemon juice
- 3g gelatin
- 1g sugar

Baked Pears

Preparation Steps:

1. Preheat the ninja air fryer device to 205° C.
2. Scoop out a portion of the centre of the pears to accommodate the oatmeal crumble.
3. Drizzle the insides of the pears with two tablespoons of melted butter and top with cinnamon sugar.
4. Combine the Light brown sugar, cinnamon, oats, almonds, and a bit of salt in a medium mixing basin.
5. Pour in the rest of the melted butter and toss until evenly covered.
6. Cook the pear halves in the preheated ninja air fryer for approximately 35 to 40 minutes, or until the pears become completely tender.
7. Serve warm with a little scoop of vanilla ice cream on top.

Ingredients:

- Four ripe pears
- 120g melted butter
- 2g cinnamon sugar
- 90g Old-fashioned rolled oats
- 35g finely chopped almonds
- 55g Light brown sugar
- 3g ground cinnamon
- Sea salt

 Prep + Cooking Time: 50 mins

 Portions: 7

Made in the USA
Las Vegas, NV
16 September 2023

77674069R00044